# THE ESSENTIAL WEDDING PLANNER

*Every Checklist, Tool, and Tip Needed to Plan the Perfect Day*

Mariah Grumet Humbert

*The wedding of*

_____

and

_____

# Contents

INTRODUCTION • 6

## inspiration

Wedding Ideas • 10
Ceremony Mood Board • 12
Reception Mood Board • 14
Floral Elements • 16
Determining Our Wedding Style • 18
Nonnegotiables • 20
Our Nonnegotiables • 21

## budget

Budget Game Plan • 24
Traditional Expense Chart • 25
Budget Savings Plan • 26
Budget Tracker • 28
Payment Tracker • 34

## timeline

Wedding Timeline Checklist • 38
Month To-Do Lists • 42

## venue

Our Venue Preferences • 62
Comparing Venues • 64
Our Venue List • 66
Our Chosen Venue • 72

## vendors

Vendor Questions • 76
Vendor Research • 82
Booked Vendors • 84

## guests

Approaching the Guest List • 88
Our Category List • 89
Our Invitation List • 90

## attendants

Selecting Our Wedding Party • 98
Our Wedding Party Costs • 100

## stationery

A Complete Stationery List • 104
Save-the-Dates • 105
Invitation Suite Components • 106
Stationery Ideas • 108
Save-the-Date and Invitation Count • 110
Final Stationery Counts • 116
Wedding Website • 118
Notes • 119

## registry

Creating the Perfect Registry • 122
Registry Wish List • 123

## attire

Wedding Attire • 130
Couple's Wedding Attire • 131
Wedding Party Attire • 138

## accommodations

Hotel Block Options • 142
Accommodations for Distinguished Guests • 144
Transportation Details • 146

## rehearsal

Rehearsal Venue Options • 150
Rehearsal Vendors • 152
Seating Arrangements • 154
Ceremony Rehearsal • 160
Rehearsal Dinner Schedule • 162

## ceremony

Questions to Consider • 166
Ceremony Plans • 167
Processional Order • 169
Vows • 170
Ceremony Schedule • 172

## reception

Traditions and Customs • 178
Cocktail Hour • 180
Dinner Menu • 182
Music Choices • 184
Speeches/Toasts • 186
Cake • 188
Reception Schedule • 190
Seating Arrangements • 192

## schedule

Traditional Wedding Schedule • 200
Our Wedding Schedule • 202

## events

Other Events Game Plan • 206

## post-wedding

Post-Wedding To-Do List • 212
Thank-You Notes • 213
Gift List • 214
Honeymoon Planning • 218
Honeymoon Itinerary • 219

**LOVE, LAUGHTER, AND HAPPILY EVER AFTER!** • 220

**NOTES** • 222

# Introduction

Dear Reader,

It is time to plan the day that you have likely been dreaming about for a big part of your life: your wedding! May I begin by saying congratulations to the special couple! As your guide throughout this entire planner, please allow me to introduce myself. I am Mariah Grumet Humbert, a New York City-based etiquette trainer, founder of Old Soul Etiquette, and author of the modern wedding etiquette book *What Do I Do?* I am honored to play a small part in your big day.

There is a good chance that as you open this planner, you are filled with a multitude of emotions. Excitement, nervousness, overwhelm, and joy, to name a few. You may still be in your post-engagement bliss, excited and ready to get started with the planning, or you may not know where to start. You may have a pretty clear vision of what you want your wedding day to look like or you may not have a clue at all. I want to tell you that every single thing you are feeling right now is valid, and wherever you are in your planning process is wonderful! Planning a wedding is one of those things where excitement, joy, stress, and overwhelm can coexist.

The goal of this planner is to provide you with tools, tips, encouragement, and guidance to help make wedding planning more approachable and organized. With this, my hope is that you can truly focus on the little details and the thrill of this extremely special chapter of your life. This planner will guide you through each step of the planning process from beginning to end so you can bring your dream and vision to life.

Weddings come in all shapes and sizes depending on each individual couple, their relationships, family, culture, and preferences. While this planner will serve as a guide, I welcome you to cross things out that don't apply to your experience, add things that do, and make any changes you deem necessary or important to best suit your vision and experience. This is your wedding, after all!

 I wish you, the soon-to-be newlyweds, a lifetime of happiness and good health together.

Let's get started with the planning, shall we?

Cheers!

*Marial Krumet Humbert*

# Inspiration

This section is dedicated to exploring your desired wedding style and vision. Jot down any initial ideas that come to mind, collect inspirational photographs, make a list of things you liked at other weddings you've attended, and create mood boards. Once you have a better idea of what your dream wedding looks like, you'll be able to start bringing that vision to life. Use this section to organize your ideas, and figure out your nonnegotiables. Allow yourself to be creative!

## ⇔ Wedding Ideas ⇔

Use the following pages to write down your and your partner's initial wedding ideas, inspirations, and thoughts.

## ❖ Ceremony Mood Board ❖

Use this space to create a collage of inspirations and photos for your ceremony.

## ❖ Reception Mood Board ❖

Use this space to create a collage of inspirations and photos for your reception.

## ❧ Floral Elements ❧

Use this space for specific ideas regarding your floral design. You can include things such as color schemes, types of flowers, and any other design elements you have in mind.

_____
_____
_____
_____
_____
_____
_____
_____
_____
_____
_____
_____
_____
_____
_____

## ❧ Determining Our Wedding Style ❧

Now that you have collected some big-picture ideas, use these questions to help you and your partner determine your wedding style.

1. What size wedding do we want to have?
   - ○ Extra Small (approximately 15–25 people)
   - ○ Small (approximately 25–75 people)
   - ○ Medium (approximately 75–150 people)
   - ○ Large (approximately 150–250 people)
   - ○ Extra Large (approximately 250+ people)

2. In what season do we picture ourselves getting married?
   - ○ Winter
   - ○ Spring
   - ○ Summer
   - ○ Fall

3. What type of venue do we want?
   - ○ Banquet Hall
   - ○ Beach
   - ○ Backyard
   - ○ Hotel
   - ○ House of Worship
   - ○ Country Club or Social Club
   - ○ Museum
   - ○ Restaurant/Bar/Lounge
   - ○ Historic Landmark
   - ○ Park
   - ○ Mansion/Castle, Special Home Rental
   - ○ Vineyard, Winery, or Brewery
   - ○ Barn
   - ○ Garden
   - ○ Art Gallery, Book Store, etc.
   - ○ Community Center
   - ○ Other _____

4. What style of wedding do we want to have? (Check all that apply.)
   - ○ Traditional
   - ○ Modern
   - ○ Rustic
   - ○ Vintage/Retro
   - ○ Bohemian
   - ○ Romantic
   - ○ Tropical/Nautical
   - ○ Art Deco
   - ○ Whimsical and Colorful
   - ○ Theme
   - ○ Cultural/Religious/Ethnic
   - ○ Other _____

5. What is our desired color palette?
   - ○ Neutrals/Earth Tones
   - ○ Black and White
   - ○ Metallics
   - ○ Seasonal Colors
   - ○ Pastels
   - ○ Bright Colors
   - ○ Jewel Tones
   - ○ Other _____

6. How formal do we want the dress code for our wedding to be?
   - ○ Casual
   - ○ Semi-formal
   - ○ Cocktail
   - ○ Formal
   - ○ Black-Tie
   - ○ Black-Tie Optional
   - ○ White-Tie
   - ○ Theme

7. Check off any other high-level elements you and your partner envision for your wedding.
   - ○ Buffet
   - ○ Sit-down, Plated Dinner
   - ○ Family Style
   - ○ Band
   - ○ DJ
   - ○ Playlist
   - ○ Indoor Wedding
   - ○ Outdoor Wedding
   - ○ Private Ceremony
   - ○ Multiple Ceremonies
   - ○ Religious Ceremony
   - ○ Destination Venue
   - ○ Local Venue

# ❖ Nonnegotiables ❖

Before you jump into creating your budget, you need to know what elements of your wedding are absolute priorities. Your list of nonnegotiables will help you and your partner allocate the proper funds to the things you consider absolute. Having a clear direction on your priorities will help you make easier decisions going forward.

You and your partner may have different priorities, so this exercise will likely require a bit of compromise. Below is a list of example nonnegotiables. Use it as a guide to create your own list and be sure to refer to your list throughout your planning journey.

### ❖ NONNEGOTIABLES EXAMPLES ❖

- Two ceremonies (interfaith marriage)
- Large venue
- Summer wedding
- Saturday evening
- Videographer
- Sit-down dinner (no buffet)
- Top-shelf, open bar

## ❖ Our Nonnegotiables ❖

- _____
- _____
- _____
- _____
- _____
- _____
- _____
- _____
- _____
- _____
- _____
- _____
- _____
- _____
- _____
- _____
- _____
- _____

# Budget

Now that you have some initial thoughts on your wedding vision and style, it's time to create your wedding budget. Your budget is likely the component of planning that will be the deciding factor for the rest of the details to fall into place. It's important to acknowledge that, like many other aspects of wedding planning, each couple's journey and preferences will be different, therefore, so will their wedding budget. This section will guide you through creating your budget, keeping track of expenses, and figuring out who will be responsible for paying for what.

# Budget Game Plan

Let's discuss the three main steps to follow when creating your wedding budget. My advice is to avoid committing to anything until you have your budget well sorted out.

### Step 1: A Conversation with Your Partner

The first step to laying out your budget is to discuss everything with your partner. It is imperative that you are both on the same page and have a general idea of how much things will cost before bringing anyone else into the conversation. The following are questions to consider with your partner.

- What is the general cost of things (venues, vendors, etc.) for the wedding style we both want to have in the area we want to have it in?
- How much do we have set aside (or can put aside) for wedding expenses?
- What is our plan for saving going forward?
- Did any of our loved ones already offer or say something about contributing to the budget?
- Are we planning on asking anyone else to contribute to the budget?

### Step 2: A Conversation with Contributing Loved Ones

If you are speaking to loved ones about contributing to your wedding, it's important to be respectful, straightforward, patient, and confident when asking them if and how much they can contribute. Set intentional time for the conversation, ensuring the only people who are present for the conversation are those who should be and it is the right time and place. Finally, set realistic expectations. You may not get the answer you want. Be flexible and willing to compromise!

### Step 3: Extensive Research and Final Game Plan

The last step to creating your wedding budget is to finalize your research, determine your big number, and create your game plan. Once you know the budget you are working with, you can begin to do more extensive research and ultimately estimate what each cost breakdown will be. If something on your nonnegotiables comes in slightly higher than you estimated, you can move some numbers around. The following charts will help you through this final step.

## ❧ Traditional Expense Chart ☙

Below is a traditional expense chart that you can use as a guide to determine who may pay for what.

| BRIDE'S FAMILY | GROOM'S FAMILY | WEDDING PARTY |
|---|---|---|
| Wedding Ceremony and Reception | Marriage License and Officiant Fee | Bachelorette Party: Maid of Honor and Bridesmaids |
| Bride's Attire | Rehearsal Dinner/ Welcome Party | Bachelor Party: Best Man and Groomsmen |
| Large Vendors (Stationery, Florals, Photo/Video, Catering, etc.) | Bride's Rings | Wedding Party Attire |
| Groom's Ring | Groom's Attire | Portions of Bridal/ Wedding Shower |
| Wedding Transportation | Honeymoon Expenses | Transportation/ Accommodations |

## ❖ Budget Savings Plan ❖

Outside contributions $_____ + our savings $_____ = $_____

Our estimated wedding cost $_____ — all contributions $_____ = what we have left to save $_____

**PLANNING TIP:** *It's important to leave a cushion for costs that may come up or change in the planning process, such as taxes, administrative fees, vendor tips, and more.*

**Our saving game plan:**

_____

_____

_____

_____

_____

_____

_____

_____

_____

_____

_____

_____

_____

## ⤝ Budget Tracker ⤞

**Total Wedding Budget:** $ _____

**PLANNING TIP:** *Make sure to add all taxes and fees when including actual costs.*

### CEREMONY, COCKTAIL HOUR, AND RECEPTION

| ITEM | BUDGET | ACTUAL COST | PAYEE | NOTES |
|---|---|---|---|---|
| Wedding Planner | | | | |
| Venue | | | | |
| Officiant | | | | |
| Catering | | | | |
| Cocktail Hour | | | | |
| Bar/Drinks | | | | |
| Cake | | | | |
| Rentals | | | | |
| Hair and Makeup | | | | |

| | | | | |
|---|---|---|---|---|
| Photography | | | | |
| Videography | | | | |
| Other | | | | |

## DÉCOR

| ITEM | BUDGET | ACTUAL COST | PAYEE | NOTES |
|---|---|---|---|---|
| All Florals | | | | |
| Additional Decor | | | | |
| Additional Table/Chair Decor | | | | |
| Lighting | | | | |
| Other | | | | |

**ENTERTAINMENT**

| ITEM | BUDGET | ACTUAL COST | PAYEE | NOTES |
|---|---|---|---|---|
| DJ | | | | |
| Live Band | | | | |
| Sound System | | | | |
| Dance Floor | | | | |
| Hired Entertainment (e.g., dancers, cigar rollers, etc.) | | | | |
| Other | | | | |

## WEDDING ATTIRE AND BEAUTY

| ITEM | BUDGET | ACTUAL COST | PAYEE | NOTES |
|---|---|---|---|---|
| Partner 1 Attire and Accessories | | | | |
| Partner 2 Attire and Accessories | | | | |
| Alterations | | | | |
| Wedding Party Attire | | | | |

## GIFTS AND RINGS

| ITEM | BUDGET | ACTUAL COST | PAYEE | NOTES |
|---|---|---|---|---|
| Rings | | | | |
| Gifts for Wedding Party | | | | |
| Gifts for Parents | | | | |
| Wedding Favors | | | | |
| Other | | | | |

**STATIONERY**

| ITEM | BUDGET | ACTUAL COST | PAYEE | NOTES |
|---|---|---|---|---|
| Save-the-Dates | | | | |
| Invitations | | | | |
| Thank-You Cards | | | | |
| Day-of Stationery (e.g. menus, programs, place cards, etc.) | | | | |
| Other | | | | |

**ACCOMMODATIONS**

| ITEM | BUDGET | ACTUAL COST | PAYEE | NOTES |
|---|---|---|---|---|
| Hotel | | | | |
| Transportation | | | | |
| Other | | | | |

**OTHER EVENTS**

| ITEM | BUDGET | ACTUAL COST | PAYEE | NOTES |
|---|---|---|---|---|
| Engagement Party | | | | |
| Rehearsal | | | | |
| Welcome Party | | | | |
| Bach Parties | | | | |
| Other | | | | |

**MISCELLANEOUS COSTS**

| ITEM | BUDGET | ACTUAL COST | PAYEE | NOTES |
|---|---|---|---|---|
| Cost "Cushion" | | | | |

**BUDGET CHANGES**

| ITEM | BUDGET | ACTUAL COST | PAYEE | NOTES |
|---|---|---|---|---|
| | | | | |

## ◆◆ Payment Tracker ◆◆

Use these pages to keep track of deposits you've made and what is still owed.

| ITEM | DEPOSIT AMOUNT | STILL OWED | PAYMENT DUE |
|------|----------------|------------|-------------|
|      |                |            |             |
|      |                |            |             |
|      |                |            |             |
|      |                |            |             |
|      |                |            |             |
|      |                |            |             |
|      |                |            |             |
|      |                |            |             |
|      |                |            |             |
|      |                |            |             |
|      |                |            |             |
|      |                |            |             |

| ITEM | DEPOSIT AMOUNT | STILL OWED | PAYMENT DUE |
|---|---|---|---|
|  |  |  |  |
|  |  |  |  |
|  |  |  |  |
|  |  |  |  |
|  |  |  |  |
|  |  |  |  |
|  |  |  |  |
|  |  |  |  |
|  |  |  |  |
|  |  |  |  |
|  |  |  |  |
|  |  |  |  |
|  |  |  |  |

# Timeline

....................

Your individual wedding planning timeline will be dependent on things such as your budget, desired wedding date, desired venue availability, and wedding style. This section will provide an example of a wedding timeline with checklists as well as space to keep track of important dates (such as venue tours, special appointments, payment schedules, etc.), followed by pages for monthly to-do lists. Change, remove, and update anything that does not fit with your wedding style.

# ❖ Wedding Timeline Checklist ❖

### 12+ Months To Go

- ○ Determine your budget and have all necessary financial conversations
- ○ Decide on the type of wedding, including any additional celebrations, you want to have (style, formality, season, etc.)
- ○ Develop your initial guest list
- ○ Create your venue (ceremony and reception) wish list and schedule tours
- ○ Secure your ceremony and reception venues and wedding date
- ○ Begin researching and contacting vendors
- ○ Hire a wedding planner (if you are choosing to use one)

### 10–11 Months To Go

- ○ Hire time-sensitive or high-demand vendors (e.g., photographer, band, caterer, etc.) and your officiant
- ○ Hire and begin planning with your stationery designer
- ○ Start researching and scheduling shopping appointments for wedding gown, if applicable (traditional gowns often require a longer lead time)
- ○ Ask people to be part of your wedding party
- ○ Finalize your guest list

### 7–9 Months To Go

- ○ Create your wedding website
- ○ Register for gifts
- ○ Purchase any additional attire for you and your partner (suits, tuxedos, party dresses, etc.)
- ○ Create, order, and send your save-the-dates
- ○ Begin thinking about the design of your invitations
- ○ Finish booking any vendors that you have not secured already
- ○ Select attire for your wedding party

- ○ Schedule cake tastings and order wedding cake
- ○ Book additional venues for rehearsal dinners, welcome parties, etc.
- ○ Book hotel blocks or necessary accommodations for your out-of-town guests

## 4–6 Months To Go

- ○ Purchase wedding bands
- ○ Book any necessary transportation for you and/or your guests
- ○ Start scheduling hair and makeup trials
- ○ Choose and order your invitations
- ○ Schedule wedding gown/attire alteration appointments, if applicable
- ○ Secure any rentals you will be using for the wedding
- ○ Begin any special beauty and self-care regimens
- ○ Meet with your caterer or venue to create your menu and schedule food tasting
- ○ Plan details for other events, such as a rehearsal dinner or welcome party
- ○ Purchase any décor
- ○ Select music for wedding day
- ○ Begin planning your honeymoon if you are leaving right after your wedding

## 2–3 Months To Go

- ○ Send out wedding invitations
- ○ Finalize hair and makeup trials, if applicable
- ○ Check in with your vendors to see if they need anything from you from a planning perspective
- ○ Confirm outstanding details and remaining payment schedules with vendors
- ○ Finalize accessories for you, your partner, and your wedding party
- ○ Make your pre-wedding beauty appointments
- ○ Finalize attire alterations
- ○ Purchase any gifts you will be giving your parents, wedding party, partner, etc. over your wedding weekend
- ○ Plan for speeches/toasts
- ○ Begin planning your ceremony
- ○ Finalize your day-of stationery (e.g., menus, place cards, signs, programs, etc.)

## 1 Month To Go

- ◯ Obtain your marriage license
- ◯ Finalize your ceremony including vows, readings, etc.
- ◯ Pick up wedding attire
- ◯ Contact guests who have not responded if deadline for RSVP has passed
- ◯ Create seating chart
- ◯ Visit your venue one last time before your wedding date to tie up any loose ends
- ◯ Fit in the last of your self-care regimen leading up to the wedding
- ◯ Create a schedule for your wedding weekend and share it/confirm it with your vendors, your venue's manager/point of contact, your wedding party, and your family

## 1–2 Weeks To Go

- ◯ Provide your venue/caterer and any other necessary vendors with final counts, allergies, etc.
- ◯ Make sure that everyone in your party, family, vendors, etc. have the wedding schedule and know what's happening and when
- ◯ Finalize your seating chart and place cards once all RSVPs come through
- ◯ Pack your overnight bag and get your wedding wardrobe and accessories together
- ◯ Put remaining payments and vendor tips in labeled envelopes (or complete online)
- ◯ Prepare your day-of emergency kit (page 221)
- ◯ Complete final beauty treatments, such as hairstyling, manicure, pedicure, eyebrow waxing, etc.

## The Day Before

- ○ If you are decorating the venue yourself, begin the setup process today if you are able to
- ○ Take inventory of everything you need for the big day and take care of any final details
- ○ Confirm the wedding timeline one last time with everyone in your party
- ○ Enjoy your rehearsal and rehearsal dinner
- ○ Take some time for yourself for self-care

## The Big Day

- ○ Ensure that you have given yourself enough time to get ready
- ○ Eat a hearty breakfast and stay hydrated
- ○ Make sure you have your emergency wedding kit (see page 221)
- ○ Delegate tasks as needed
- ○ Stay flexible and enjoy yourself

## Other

- _____
- _____
- _____
- _____
- _____
- _____
- _____
- _____
- _____

# Month _____

**To-Do List**

- _____
- _____
- _____
- _____
- _____
- _____
- _____
- _____
- _____
- _____
- _____
- _____
- _____
- _____
- _____
- _____
- _____
- _____

# Month _____

**To-Do List**

- _____
- _____
- _____
- _____
- _____
- _____
- _____
- _____
- _____
- _____
- _____
- _____
- _____
- _____
- _____
- _____
- _____
- _____
- _____

# Month _____

**To-Do List**

- _____
- _____
- _____
- _____
- _____
- _____
- _____
- _____
- _____
- _____
- _____
- _____
- _____
- _____
- _____
- _____
- _____

# Month _____

**To-Do List**

- _____
- _____
- _____
- _____
- _____
- _____
- _____
- _____
- _____
- _____
- _____
- _____
- _____
- _____
- _____
- _____
- _____
- _____
- _____

# Month _____

**To-Do List**

- _____
- _____
- _____
- _____
- _____
- _____
- _____
- _____
- _____
- _____
- _____
- _____
- _____
- _____
- _____
- _____

# Month _____

**To-Do List**

- _____
- _____
- _____
- _____
- _____
- _____
- _____
- _____
- _____
- _____
- _____
- _____
- _____
- _____
- _____
- _____
- _____
- _____
- _____

# Month _____

**To-Do List**

- _____
- _____
- _____
- _____
- _____
- _____
- _____
- _____
- _____
- _____
- _____
- _____
- _____
- _____
- _____
- _____
- _____

# Month _____

**To-Do List**

- _____
- _____
- _____
- _____
- _____
- _____
- _____
- _____
- _____
- _____
- _____
- _____
- _____
- _____
- _____
- _____
- _____
- _____

**Month** _____

**To-Do List**

- _____
- _____
- _____
- _____
- _____
- _____
- _____
- _____
- _____
- _____
- _____
- _____
- _____
- _____
- _____
- _____
- _____

# Month _____

**To-Do List**

- _____
- _____
- _____
- _____
- _____
- _____
- _____
- _____
- _____
- _____
- _____
- _____
- _____
- _____
- _____
- _____
- _____
- _____
- _____

# Month _____

**To-Do List**

- _____
- _____
- _____
- _____
- _____
- _____
- _____
- _____
- _____
- _____
- _____
- _____
- _____
- _____
- _____
- _____
- _____

# Month _____

**To-Do List**

- _____
- _____
- _____
- _____
- _____
- _____
- _____
- _____
- _____
- _____
- _____
- _____
- _____
- _____
- _____
- _____
- _____

# Month _____

**To-Do List**

- _____
- _____
- _____
- _____
- _____
- _____
- _____
- _____
- _____
- _____
- _____
- _____
- _____
- _____
- _____
- _____
- _____

# Month _____

**To-Do List**

- _____
- _____
- _____
- _____
- _____
- _____
- _____
- _____
- _____
- _____
- _____
- _____
- _____
- _____
- _____
- _____
- _____

# Month _____

**To-Do List**

- _____
- _____
- _____
- _____
- _____
- _____
- _____
- _____
- _____
- _____
- _____
- _____
- _____
- _____
- _____
- _____
- _____
- _____

# Month _____

**To-Do List**

- _____
- _____
- _____
- _____
- _____
- _____
- _____
- _____
- _____
- _____
- _____
- _____
- _____
- _____
- _____
- _____
- _____
- _____

# Month _____

**To-Do List**

- _____
- _____
- _____
- _____
- _____
- _____
- _____
- _____
- _____
- _____
- _____
- _____
- _____
- _____
- _____
- _____
- _____
- _____

# Month _____

**To-Do List**

- _____
- _____
- _____
- _____
- _____
- _____
- _____
- _____
- _____
- _____
- _____
- _____
- _____
- _____
- _____
- _____
- _____

# Venue

............................

Booking your venue is likely the most time-sensitive decision you will have to make, especially if you have a specific list of places or a special date in mind. You will not be able to truly finalize your guest list or begin booking your vendors until your venue is secured. You may have your wedding venue type in mind, and you may want to tour a few different ones! Use this section to begin considering some important factors to help you narrow down your venue.

## ❧ Our Venue Preferences ❧

Our desired wedding date or timeframe is _____.

What type of venue do we prefer for our wedding? Check all that apply.

- ○ Banquet Hall
- ○ Beach
- ○ Backyard
- ○ Hotel
- ○ House of Worship
- ○ Country Club or Social Club
- ○ Museum
- ○ Restaurant/Bar/Lounge
- ○ Historic Landmark
- ○ Park
- ○ Mansion/Castle
- ○ Special Home Rental
- ○ Vineyard, Winery, or Brewery
- ○ Barn
- ○ Garden
- ○ Art Gallery, Book Store, etc.
- ○ Community Center
- ○ Other _____

Do we want the ceremony and reception to be in the same location or separate locations? Circle what applies.

**SAME LOCATION** or **SEPARATE LOCATIONS**

If separate locations, list out a few options for locations here:

- _____
- _____
- _____
- _____

Are we willing to save money in another area to book our dream venue?

_____

_____

_____

_____

If so, list out which areas you're willing to sacrifice a bit for your venue.

- _____
- _____
- _____
- _____
- _____
- _____
- _____
- _____
- _____
- _____

# Comparing Venues

As you begin researching venues and deciding where you want to tour, be sure to look over the venue's reviews, photographs, social media channels, etc. Prepare your questions ahead of time to help you get the most out of your correspondence and tours. Here are some suggestions to ask yourselves and the venues. Add any other questions that you and your partner feel are important to ask as well!

**PLANNING TIP:** *Many couples find it helpful to create a separate email account that they can dedicate to their communication with vendors and wedding planning.*

- Does this venue cost fit into our budget? Are there different packages available?
- Does this venue match the overall desired look and feel of our wedding?
- What is the proximity to the ceremony venue (if you are getting married off-site)?
- How many people can the venue comfortably accommodate?
- What is included versus what will we have to bring in?
- What is the general location of the venue? Are there accommodations nearby for our out-of-town guests?
- How accessible is the venue for our guests, such as ramps, elevators, parking, accessible lighting, etc.?
- Does the venue have any limitations or restrictions such as timing, noise ordinances, décor, etc.?
- Do you get exclusivity of the venue on your wedding day?
- Are there designated "getting ready" areas for the couple, family, and wedding party?
- Does the venue have a particular layout for seating, or is it flexible?
- What is the restroom situation?
- If it is an outdoor venue or partially indoor, partially outdoor, what is the weather plan?

**Other Questions**

- _____
- _____
- _____
- _____
- _____
- _____
- _____
- _____
- _____
- _____
- _____
- _____
- _____
- _____
- _____
- _____

**PLANNING TIP:** *For a destination wedding, you may have to give a bit of extra attention to considering the general location (safety, transportation options, etc.), guest accommodations, travel requirements, etc.*

# ❖ Our Venue List ❖

| |
|---|
| Venue Name: |
| Location: |
| Contact: |
| Cost: |
| Available Packages: |
| Availability: |
| Allows Children: |
| Accommodations: |
| Restrictions: |
| Accessibility: |
| Tour Notes: |

| | |
|---|---|
| Venue Name: | |
| Location: | |
| Contact: | |
| Cost: | |
| Available Packages: | |
| Availability: | |
| Allows Children: | |
| Accommodations: | |
| Restrictions: | |
| Accessibility: | |
| Tour Notes: | |

## ❖ Our Venue List ❖

| | |
|---|---|
| Venue Name: | |
| Location: | |
| Contact: | |
| Cost: | |
| Available Packages: | |
| Availability: | |
| Allows Children: | |
| Accommodations: | |
| Restrictions: | |
| Accessibility: | |
| Tour Notes: | |

| | |
|---|---|
| Venue Name: | |
| Location: | |
| Contact: | |
| Cost: | |
| Available Packages: | |
| Availability: | |
| Allows Children: | |
| Accommodations: | |
| Restrictions: | |
| Accessibility: | |
| Tour Notes: | |

## ❖ Our Venue List ❖

| | |
|---|---|
| Venue Name: | |
| Location: | |
| Contact: | |
| Cost: | |
| Available Packages: | |
| Availability: | |
| Allows Children: | |
| Accommodations: | |
| Restrictions: | |
| Accessibility: | |
| Tour Notes: | |

| |
|---|
| Venue Name: |
| Location: |
| Contact: |
| Cost: |
| Available Packages: |
| Availability: |
| Allows Children: |
| Accommodations: |
| Restrictions: |
| Accessibility: |
| Tour Notes: |

# ⇸ Our Chosen Venue ⇸

This table is designated for your chosen venue. Not only will this give you one place to visually see the information, but also, it's the magic chart that will help you determine your vendor list!

**Venue Name** _____

| ITEM/SERVICE | VENUE COVERS | NEED TO OUTSOURCE<br>*(Hire vendor/rent)* |
|---|---|---|
| Food | | |
| Beverage | | |
| Servers, Bartenders, etc. | | |
| Cake | | |

| ITEM/SERVICE | VENUE COVERS | NEED TO OUTSOURCE *(Hire vendor/rent)* |
|---|---|---|
| Tables and Linens | | |
| Audio and Visual | | |
| Setup/Breakdown Crew | | |
| Parking | | |
| Other | | |

# Vendors

...................

Now, it's time for us to move on to talk about the group of people who are going to help put the puzzle pieces together: your vendors. It's never too early to start booking your vendors to ensure the ones you want to work with are available on your wedding date. Keep in mind that every booking should be secured with a thorough contract signed by both parties. Use this section to help you determine what questions to ask and record your vendor research.

# ⇥ Vendor Questions ⇤

Some vendors are more time sensitive, and you will want to consider booking them first. This list includes the wedding planner/coordinator, hair stylist, makeup artist, officiant, videographer, photographer, florist, catering, and music vendors. Here are lists of suggested questions to ask vendors. You can add any additional questions you deem necessary as well!

**PLANNING TIP:** *Plan to feed and tip any vendors who are present with you throughout your wedding day, such as makeup artists or hair stylists, floral/rental setup staff, ceremony officiant, musicians/DJ, and more. You will want to coordinate this with your venue and include it in your budget.*

### Questions to Ask *All* Vendors:

- Are you available on our wedding date?
- What pricing and packages do you offer?
- What is your cancellation policy?
- Do you have insurance and the proper licenses?
- Do you have a clause in your contract regarding what measures will be taken if you have to cancel?
- Where can we find photos, videos, and/or reviews of your work?
- What is your service fee, administrative fee, tax, etc.?
- Have you worked with our venue before?
- Have you worked with a couple with our wedding style before (e.g., interfaith, religious, cultural, same sex, etc.)?

### Wedding Planner/Coordinator

- What exactly do your services include?
- Do you have a list of preferred vendors to work with?
- What does the planning timeline and process look like when working with you?
- How often will we meet and what is your preferred communication style?
- How many people do you bring with you on the day of, if any?

### Photographer

- How would you describe your photography and editing style?
- How many people/cameras will be photographing on the day of?
- What type of equipment do you use to shoot your photos?
- How do you work with couples to ensure they are comfortable in front of a camera?
- Do you send sneak peeks soon after the wedding?
- How long does it take for the photos to be returned after the wedding?
- How many photos should we expect to receive?
- How many hours of coverage do you typically shoot?
- Is an album or prints included in the price?
- How do you navigate posting your work on your social media and website?

### Videographer

- How would you describe your videography and editing style?
- How many people/cameras will be recording on the day of?
- What type of equipment do you use to shoot your videos?
- How do you work with couples to ensure they are comfortable in front of a camera?
- Do you send sneak peeks soon after the wedding?
- How long does it take for the video to be returned after the wedding?
- How long are the videos in duration?
- How many hours of coverage do you typically shoot?
- What is included in our fee (e.g., sneak peek, trailer, full video, unedited footage, etc.)?

### Florist

- How would you describe your floral design style?
- What décor are you able to provide versus what we will have to plan to outsource? How is décor factored into the cost (e.g., candles, vases, etc.)?
- Do you take on more than one wedding on a particular day?
- Where do you source your flowers from?
- How do you source flowers that are not in season?
- What are your setup and breakdown processes?
- Are you able to provide/set up florals for our ceremony and reception venues?
- Do you provide mock-ups for sketches?

### Caterer/Bartender

- What will you need at our venue to successfully cater there?
- Do you take on more than one wedding or special event on a particular day?
- Do your packages include rentals (linens, serving ware, silverware, dishes, glassware, etc.) and/or service staff?
- Do you offer bartending services?
- Do you offer both buffet and sit-down dinner service?
- Do you allow your clients to customize a menu?
- Do you offer a menu tasting?
- How do you handle dietary restrictions and allergies?
- What are the portion sizes?
- Do you include a cake in your services?
- Is the food made on-site or brought to the site already made?
- What do your setup/cleanup processes look like?
- When do you need a final guest count?

### Officiant

- How long is your average ceremony?
- Are your ceremonies customized? If so, how do you incorporate the couple in the planning process?
- Are you willing to participate in our rehearsal?
- What do you typically wear when officiating a wedding?
- Do you allow couples to write and say their own vows? If so, do you provide guidance on this?
- Do you provide advice on processional orders, ceremony flow, etc.?
- Do you help us obtain our marriage license?

### Hair and Makeup

- Do you offer services for the bridal party, family, etc. in addition to the bride(s)?
- How many people do you bring with you to assist?
- How long should each person take for hair and makeup?
- What products do you use?
- Do you bring all of your own products and tools?

- Are hair and makeup trials included as a part of the service?
- Do you have travel fees?
- What are your space requirements?
- Do you offer services for other wedding-related events, such as a shower or rehearsal dinner?
- Have you worked with someone with a similar hair type and skin tone/type before?

## Transportation

- What type of vehicles do you offer?
- Is it possible to offer multiple times to return guests back to the designated hotel?
- Do you allow food and beverages on your vehicles?
- Do you offer special transportation for the couple only or the couple plus immediate family and/or wedding party?
- Are we allowed to operate the vehicle (for special "drive away" rentals)?

## Music

- What genre(s) of music are you able to perform/play?
- Are we able to choose our song list?
- Are you able to learn a new song(s) if we have a special request(s)?
- Do you bring all of your own equipment?
- How many breaks do you take during an event?
- What are your audio or visual requirements?
- Can we hire a different number of musicians for each event (e.g., the full band for the reception, a few pieces for cocktail hour, a singer plus one instrument for the ceremony)?
- Do you take song requests from the guests the night of the event?
- Are you able to act as our emcee for the evening?

## Stationery

- What is your full list of stationery offerings from save the dates to invitations to day-of stationery?
- Do you offer customization?
- What is your working timeline for all stationery needs?
- What does your proofing process look like?

- What printing techniques, special details, additions, and design elements do you offer/specialize in?
- Do you offer large signage?
- Do you assemble invitations?
- Do you have a calligrapher in-house?
- Do you print in-house?

### Cake

- Do you accommodate allergies or dietary restrictions?
- What is your delivery/setup process?
- How far in advance do you make the cake?
- How big a cake do you recommend for our wedding size?
- Are there any techniques or design elements that you specialize in?
- What does the cake-tasting process look like?

### Rentals (linens, furniture, etc.)

- What is your scope of products and offerings?
- Do you deliver, set up, and take down everything we rent?
- How long are your rental periods?
- Have you done a wedding similar to ours/within our general theme before?

### Wedding Attire

- How long does it take to get attire delivered/ready (e.g., wedding gown, tuxedo, special-ordered outfit, etc.)?
- How does the alterations process work?
- Are alterations included in the overall price?

### Other

- _____
- _____
- _____
- _____

## ❖ Vendor Research ❖

| TYPE | NAME | PRICE | NOTES |
|---|---|---|---|
| *Example: Hair* | *Alyssa Smith* | *$150 per person* | *Willing to travel* |
| | | | |
| | | | |
| | | | |
| | | | |
| | | | |
| | | | |
| | | | |
| | | | |
| | | | |
| | | | |
| | | | |
| | | | |

| TYPE | NAME | PRICE | NOTES |
|------|------|-------|-------|
| | | | |
| | | | |
| | | | |
| | | | |
| | | | |
| | | | |
| | | | |
| | | | |
| | | | |
| | | | |
| | | | |
| | | | |
| | | | |

## ❧ Booked Vendors ❧

| TYPE | NAME | PRICE | NOTES | VENUE TAKES CARE IN-HOUSE (*check mark*) |
|---|---|---|---|---|
| Planner/ Coordinator | | | | ○ |
| Photographer | | | | ○ |
| Videographer | | | | ○ |
| Florist | | | | ○ |
| Caterer | | | | ○ |
| Bartender | | | | ○ |
| Officiant | | | | ○ |

| TYPE | NAME | PRICE | NOTES | VENUE TAKES CARE IN-HOUSE (*check mark*) |
|---|---|---|---|---|
| Hair and Makeup | | | | ○ |
| Transportation | | | | ○ |
| Music | | | | ○ |
| Stationery | | | | ○ |
| Cake | | | | ○ |
| Rentals | | | | ○ |
| Other | | | | ○ |

# Guests

..................

It's that time in the planning process to decide who you want to be surrounded by on your special day! This section will guide you through creating your guest list and keeping track of who you plan on inviting, addresses, and guest notes (e.g., allergies, dietary restrictions, menu selection, etc.).

# ❧ Approaching the Guest List ❧

When creating your guest list, it is best to start by considering your venue and budget as they will determine the number of guests you will invite. While there is a good chance at least 10 percent of people will not be able to make it, you need to know that your venue is able to accommodate the full list and that you as the couple can comfortably cover the cost of the full list of invitees. You'll also want to decide if you'll be including children in your guest list. The following are suggestions for how to create and finalize your guest list.

## ❧ CATEGORIES ❧

Craft your list by categorizing the different groups of people in your lives and ranking them in level of importance and priority. That way, if you have to cut back, it's easier to determine where to go first. For example, if you have to limit guests, you may limit the number of invitees in your "work friends" category rather than your "extended family" category.

**Example Category List**

1. Immediate family
2. Extended family
3. College friends
4. Hometown friends
5. Parents' friends
6. Work friends
7. Children (if applicable)

## ❧ DETERMINING PLUS-ONES ❧

Firstly, it's important to understand the difference between a plus-one and a partner. If someone is in an established relationship, it is best to invite them along with their partner as a couple. The other person would be considered their partner, *not* their plus-one. Giving someone a plus-one or a guest insinuates that the person is not in a committed relationship and is welcome to bring a date to your wedding. It is completely up to you and your partner's preferences as to whether you decide to give plus-ones. However, you'll want to remain consistent once you figure out what works best for your wedding.

## ❖ COLLECTING ADDRESSES ❖

If you need to collect addresses, I recommend using Google Forms. You can have your guests fill out the form, and then all of the addresses are stored in one easily accessible place that you can continue to refer to for special celebrations to come.

## ❖ Our Category List ❖

1. _____
2. _____
3. _____
4. _____
5. _____
6. _____
7. _____
8. _____
9. _____
10. _____
11. _____
12. _____
13. _____
14. _____
15. _____

## ❖ Our Invitation List ❖

| NAME | ADDRESS | CATEGORY | NOTES |
|------|---------|----------|-------|
|      |         |          |       |
|      |         |          |       |
|      |         |          |       |
|      |         |          |       |
|      |         |          |       |
|      |         |          |       |
|      |         |          |       |
|      |         |          |       |
|      |         |          |       |
|      |         |          |       |
|      |         |          |       |
|      |         |          |       |
|      |         |          |       |

| NAME | ADDRESS | CATEGORY | NOTES |
|---|---|---|---|
|  |  |  |  |
|  |  |  |  |
|  |  |  |  |
|  |  |  |  |
|  |  |  |  |
|  |  |  |  |
|  |  |  |  |
|  |  |  |  |
|  |  |  |  |
|  |  |  |  |
|  |  |  |  |
|  |  |  |  |
|  |  |  |  |

## ✦ Our Invitation List ✦

| NAME | ADDRESS | CATEGORY | NOTES |
|------|---------|----------|-------|
|      |         |          |       |
|      |         |          |       |
|      |         |          |       |
|      |         |          |       |
|      |         |          |       |
|      |         |          |       |
|      |         |          |       |
|      |         |          |       |
|      |         |          |       |
|      |         |          |       |
|      |         |          |       |
|      |         |          |       |
|      |         |          |       |

| NAME | ADDRESS | CATEGORY | NOTES |
|------|---------|----------|-------|
|      |         |          |       |
|      |         |          |       |
|      |         |          |       |
|      |         |          |       |
|      |         |          |       |
|      |         |          |       |
|      |         |          |       |
|      |         |          |       |
|      |         |          |       |
|      |         |          |       |
|      |         |          |       |
|      |         |          |       |
|      |         |          |       |

## Our Invitation List

| NAME | ADDRESS | CATEGORY | NOTES |
|------|---------|----------|-------|
|      |         |          |       |
|      |         |          |       |
|      |         |          |       |
|      |         |          |       |
|      |         |          |       |
|      |         |          |       |
|      |         |          |       |
|      |         |          |       |
|      |         |          |       |
|      |         |          |       |
|      |         |          |       |
|      |         |          |       |
|      |         |          |       |

| NAME | ADDRESS | CATEGORY | NOTES |
|------|---------|----------|-------|
|      |         |          |       |
|      |         |          |       |
|      |         |          |       |
|      |         |          |       |
|      |         |          |       |
|      |         |          |       |
|      |         |          |       |
|      |         |          |       |
|      |         |          |       |
|      |         |          |       |
|      |         |          |       |
|      |         |          |       |

**Total Number** _____

# Attendants

..................

Let's give some extra attention to those potentially distinguished guests on your list: your wedding party! It is important that you set as many expectations as possible upfront so your wedding party knows what to anticipate in terms of time or financial commitment. The size of your wedding party and their specific roles are completely up to you and your partner! Use this section to keep track of who is going to be part of your big day and what they may have to contribute for the event.

# ↞ Selecting Our Wedding Party ↠

| TITLE/ROLE | NAME |
|---|---|
| Example: Maid of Honor | Example: Jane Smith |
| Example: Ring Bearer | Example: Thomas Grant |
| | |
| | |
| | |
| | |
| | |
| | |
| | |
| | |
| | |
| | |

| TITLE/ROLE | NAME |
|---|---|
|  |  |
|  |  |
|  |  |
|  |  |
|  |  |
|  |  |
|  |  |
|  |  |
|  |  |
|  |  |
|  |  |
|  |  |

**Total Number** _____

## ❖ Our Wedding Party Costs ❖

Use this chart to check off the items that you are paying for versus what you expect your wedding party to pay for. This will ensure you know what to include in your budget and help you manage financial expectations for your wedding party.

| CATEGORY | OUR COSTS | WEDDING PARTY COSTS | SPLITTING COSTS |
|---|---|---|---|
| Wedding Attire | | | |
| Other Outfits (e.g., getting-ready robes) | | | |
| Accessories | | | |
| Hair and Makeup | | | |
| Accommodations | | | |

| CATEGORY | OUR COSTS | WEDDING PARTY COSTS | SPLITTING COSTS |
| --- | --- | --- | --- |
| Transportation | | | |
| Bach Parties | | | |
| Wedding Shower/ Bridal Shower | | | |
| Other | | | |

# Stationery

.....................

Your stationery will include everything from save-the-dates to invitations to programs and everything in between. Your stationery is often one of the first things someone will get a glimpse of as it pertains to your wedding, so it's important to be really thoughtful here! In this section, you will find a complete stationery checklist, verbiage examples, wedding website tips, and ways to log all the information.

# ❖ A Complete Stationery List ❖

This list includes everything you will potentially need to plan for in terms of your wedding stationery. Check off only what applies to your wedding.

**PLANNING TIP:** *Your invitation should match the formality of your event. If your wedding is more casual, digital components could work well for you. If you are having a black-tie wedding, you may want to opt for a more formal, mailed invitation.*

- ○ Save-the-Dates
- ○ Rehearsal Dinner Invitation
- ○ Welcome Party Invitation
- ○ Bridal Luncheon Invitation
- ○ Brunch Invitation
- ○ Wedding Invitation
- ○ Reception Card
- ○ Accommodations Card
- ○ Response Card
- ○ Welcome Letters/Bag Tags
- ○ Ceremony Program
- ○ Escort Cards/Table Signs
- ○ Place Cards
- ○ Table Number Cards
- ○ Menus
- ○ Coasters/Cocktail Napkins/Labels
- ○ Guest Book
- ○ Signage
- ○ Thank-You Notes
- ○ Shower Invitation
- ○ Shower Thank-You Notes
- ○ Bachelor/Bachelorette Invitations
- ○ Other _____

## ✤ Save-the-Dates ✤

Plan to send save-the-dates at least six to eight months prior to your wedding date or nine to twelve months for a destination wedding. Your save-the-date should include verbiage that encourages your guests to save your wedding date (or multiple dates if there are multiple events involved), the general location, and a wedding website URL (if applicable).

**PLANNING TIP:** *You will want to ensure that your guest list is complete before you move into sending out any kind of stationery whether that be the save-the-dates, invitations, or both.*

**Example:**

*Kindly save the date for our wedding!*
*Gretchen & Thomas*
*May 18th, 2024*
*Newport Beach, California*
*Formal invitation to follow*

## ❧ Invitation Suite Components ❧

An invitation suite consists of every component that is sent as a part of the wedding invitation. You will want to plan to send your invitations to your guests two to three months prior to your wedding date. Remember, you may not want or need every single component! Apply what works well for your wedding style.

### 1. The Invitation

The actual invitation will be the main piece of stationery in your suite. Its purpose is to invite people to the marriage ceremony. If your entire guest list will also be invited to your reception, you will simply note "reception to follow" even if it is taking place at the same venue. The verbiage will depend on who is hosting, formality, etc., but the components that are often included on the invitation are listed below.

- The host
- The event (ceremony only versus ceremony with reception following)
- Your names as the couple
- When the event is taking place
- Where the event is taking place
- Dress code (if not specified on a details card)
- RSVP verbiage (if you are not using a separate response card)

**PLANNING TIP:** *Registry information should not go on a wedding invitation. It is, however, able to go on a shower invitation. If you choose to use a website, you can put your wedding website link on your invitation or save-the-date.*

### 2. Reception Card

A reception card is used when you are not inviting all guests to the ceremony. A reception card would look similar to the invitation, yet it is usually less formal and will only include reception details.

### 3. Response Card

Response cards typically include the response deadline, the guests' names, and whether they are able to attend. Additional information that may be requested on a response card are menu choices and allergies/dietary restrictions. Response cards should include a pre-addressed envelope with the address of whomever is collecting the responses and include postage.

### 4. Additional Details Card

An additional details card is there for you to provide any information that you would like your guests to be aware of that is not included on the actual invitation. You can include anything from the dress code to choosing to have an adult-only wedding to your wedding website URL, transportation offerings, etc.

### 5. Accommodations Card

This card would indicate a hotel room block you may have, hotel recommendations in the area, parking information, etc.

### 6. Additional Invitations to Other Events

If you are having any other events as a part of your wedding weekend such as a rehearsal dinner or welcome party, you may opt to include the invitation as a part of your wedding invitation suite.

### 7. Envelopes

Using an inner envelope is a traditional way to indicate and reiterate exactly who is invited to your wedding and adds an extra layer of protection for your invitation suite. An inner envelope would remain unsealed and only include names. On the other hand, an outer envelope will be the main envelope that includes your return address, your guests' full name(s), address, and proper postage.

## ↔ Stationery Ideas ↔

Use this space to plan out any design or wording ideas.

# ✦ Save-the-Date and Invitation Count ✦

Use this space to group guests into households and couples to see how many save-the-dates and invitations you need to send. Track what each household will receive, as not everyone may be invited to every one of your wedding events.

| NAMES (By household or couple) | ADDRESS | SAVE-THE-DATE (check mark) | WEDDING INVITATION (check mark) | OTHER EVENTS (check mark) | RSVP'D (check mark) |
|---|---|---|---|---|---|
| | | ○ | ○ | ○ | ○ |
| | | ○ | ○ | ○ | ○ |
| | | ○ | ○ | ○ | ○ |
| | | ○ | ○ | ○ | ○ |
| | | ○ | ○ | ○ | ○ |
| | | ○ | ○ | ○ | ○ |
| | | ○ | ○ | ○ | ○ |
| | | ○ | ○ | ○ | ○ |
| | | ○ | ○ | ○ | ○ |

| NAMES (By household or couple) | ADDRESS | SAVE-THE-DATE (check mark) | WEDDING INVITATION (check mark) | OTHER EVENTS (check mark) | RSVP'D (check mark) |
|---|---|---|---|---|---|
| | | ○ | ○ | ○ | ○ |
| | | ○ | ○ | ○ | ○ |
| | | ○ | ○ | ○ | ○ |
| | | ○ | ○ | ○ | ○ |
| | | ○ | ○ | ○ | ○ |
| | | ○ | ○ | ○ | ○ |
| | | ○ | ○ | ○ | ○ |
| | | ○ | ○ | ○ | ○ |
| | | ○ | ○ | ○ | ○ |
| | | ○ | ○ | ○ | ○ |
| | | ○ | ○ | ○ | ○ |
| | | ○ | ○ | ○ | ○ |

## ❧ Save-the-Date and Invitation Count ❧

| NAMES (By household or couple) | ADDRESS | SAVE-THE-DATE (check mark) | WEDDING INVITATION (check mark) | OTHER EVENTS (check mark) | RSVP'D (check mark) |
|---|---|---|---|---|---|
| | | ○ | ○ | ○ | ○ |
| | | ○ | ○ | ○ | ○ |
| | | ○ | ○ | ○ | ○ |
| | | ○ | ○ | ○ | ○ |
| | | ○ | ○ | ○ | ○ |
| | | ○ | ○ | ○ | ○ |
| | | ○ | ○ | ○ | ○ |
| | | ○ | ○ | ○ | ○ |
| | | ○ | ○ | ○ | ○ |
| | | ○ | ○ | ○ | ○ |
| | | ○ | ○ | ○ | ○ |

| NAMES (By household or couple) | ADDRESS | SAVE-THE-DATE (check mark) | WEDDING INVITATION (check mark) | OTHER EVENTS (check mark) | RSVP'D (check mark) |
|---|---|---|---|---|---|
| | | ○ | ○ | ○ | ○ |
| | | ○ | ○ | ○ | ○ |
| | | ○ | ○ | ○ | ○ |
| | | ○ | ○ | ○ | ○ |
| | | ○ | ○ | ○ | ○ |
| | | ○ | ○ | ○ | ○ |
| | | ○ | ○ | ○ | ○ |
| | | ○ | ○ | ○ | ○ |
| | | ○ | ○ | ○ | ○ |
| | | ○ | ○ | ○ | ○ |
| | | ○ | ○ | ○ | ○ |

# ❖ Save-the-Date and Invitation Count ❖

| NAMES (By household or couple) | ADDRESS | SAVE-THE-DATE (check mark) | WEDDING INVITATION (check mark) | OTHER EVENTS (check mark) | RSVP'D (check mark) |
|---|---|---|---|---|---|
| | | ○ | ○ | ○ | ○ |
| | | ○ | ○ | ○ | ○ |
| | | ○ | ○ | ○ | ○ |
| | | ○ | ○ | ○ | ○ |
| | | ○ | ○ | ○ | ○ |
| | | ○ | ○ | ○ | ○ |
| | | ○ | ○ | ○ | ○ |
| | | ○ | ○ | ○ | ○ |
| | | ○ | ○ | ○ | ○ |
| | | ○ | ○ | ○ | ○ |
| | | ○ | ○ | ○ | ○ |

| NAMES (By household or couple) | ADDRESS | SAVE-THE-DATE (check mark) | WEDDING INVITATION (check mark) | OTHER EVENTS (check mark) | RSVP'D (check mark) |
|---|---|---|---|---|---|
| | | ○ | ○ | ○ | ○ |
| | | ○ | ○ | ○ | ○ |
| | | ○ | ○ | ○ | ○ |
| | | ○ | ○ | ○ | ○ |
| | | ○ | ○ | ○ | ○ |
| | | ○ | ○ | ○ | ○ |
| | | ○ | ○ | ○ | ○ |
| | | ○ | ○ | ○ | ○ |
| | | ○ | ○ | ○ | ○ |
| | | ○ | ○ | ○ | ○ |
| | | ○ | ○ | ○ | ○ |

# ↔ Final Stationery Counts ↔

Add up the numbers from the charts on pages 110 to 115 and indicate your final number for each element. Leave a cushion by slightly overestimating the quantity of each component.

| STATIONERY TYPE | NUMBER TO ORDER |
|---|---|
| | |
| | |
| | |
| | |
| | |
| | |
| | |
| | |
| | |
| | |
| | |

| STATIONERY TYPE | NUMBER TO ORDER |
|---|---|
|  |  |
|  |  |
|  |  |
|  |  |
|  |  |
|  |  |
|  |  |
|  |  |
|  |  |
|  |  |
|  |  |
|  |  |
|  |  |
|  |  |

## ⇢ Wedding Website ⇠

Wedding websites are a newer component of wedding planning and serve the purpose of providing your guests with all of the necessary information regarding your wedding and other related events. Below you will find potential components of a wedding website. Add any other components you deem necessary.

- Home/welcome page with the date, general location, photos, and/or your story
- Schedule of events
- Travel and accommodations
- Registry
- Things to do in the area
- Wedding party
- RSVP (if you choose to do it digitally)
- Photo gallery
- Special information and additional details

**Other:**

- _____
- _____
- _____
- _____
- _____
- _____
- _____
- _____

## Notes

# Registry

Your wedding will be one of the only times as an adult where it will be acceptable (more or less!) to go through websites and catalogs and "circle" everything you desire. Your registry puts your guests at ease by allowing them to know they are getting you and your partner something you actually want and/or need. Use this section to keep an organized list of places where you want to register and gifts you want to add to your registry. This will be a section you can refer to from now until after the wedding!

# ⇇ Creating the Perfect Registry ⇉

Here are my top tips for creating the perfect wedding registry.

1. You and your partner should ask yourselves:
   - What do we want?
   - What do we need?
   - What do we already have that we want to upgrade?

2. Make sure you have a wide range of value across your items, meaning some higher ticketed items, some inexpensive items, and some items that fall in between. This will allow your guests to spend what they are comfortable spending.

3. If you want to add extra gift options to your registry, some wedding website platforms will allow you to add gift cards to various stores, airlines, food delivery services, etc.

4. If you are planning to have a honeymoon fund or cash fund, I recommend either utilizing what your wedding website provides or going through a third-party platform that is designed for these types of funds. It will be easier to manage and allows you to request a monetary gift more tactfully.

## ↔ Registry Wish List ↔

Use this list to write down anything you want to add to your registry.

| GIFT | FROM | COST |
|---|---|---|
| *Example: Wine glasses* | *Macy's* | *$50* |
| | | |
| | | |
| | | |
| | | |
| | | |
| | | |
| | | |
| | | |
| | | |
| | | |
| | | |

## Registry Wish List

| GIFT | FROM | COST |
|------|------|------|
|      |      |      |
|      |      |      |
|      |      |      |
|      |      |      |
|      |      |      |
|      |      |      |
|      |      |      |
|      |      |      |
|      |      |      |
|      |      |      |
|      |      |      |
|      |      |      |
|      |      |      |

| GIFT | FROM | COST |
|------|------|------|
|      |      |      |
|      |      |      |
|      |      |      |
|      |      |      |
|      |      |      |
|      |      |      |
|      |      |      |
|      |      |      |
|      |      |      |
|      |      |      |
|      |      |      |
|      |      |      |
|      |      |      |
|      |      |      |

## ❖ Registry Wish List ❖

| GIFT | FROM | COST |
|------|------|------|
|      |      |      |
|      |      |      |
|      |      |      |
|      |      |      |
|      |      |      |
|      |      |      |
|      |      |      |
|      |      |      |
|      |      |      |
|      |      |      |
|      |      |      |
|      |      |      |
|      |      |      |

| GIFT | FROM | COST |
|------|------|------|
|      |      |      |
|      |      |      |
|      |      |      |
|      |      |      |
|      |      |      |
|      |      |      |
|      |      |      |
|      |      |      |
|      |      |      |
|      |      |      |
|      |      |      |
|      |      |      |
|      |      |      |
|      |      |      |

# Attire

.....................

At this point, it is likely you've determined the overall formality of your wedding, including the dress code you will be indicating for your guests, or you at least have a pretty good idea depending on where you are in your planning timeline. We are going to dedicate this portion of the planner to you and your partner's attire for each event as well as how to determine attire for your wedding party or other distinguished guests.

# ❧ Wedding Attire ❧

A few special and exciting decisions await you, and those are what you plan to wear for your wedding festivities. It is likely you will make a few outfit choices depending on how many events you are planning to have (e.g., wedding shower, bach parties, rehearsal dinner, ceremony or ceremonies, etc.). I recommend starting to get an idea of your outfit plans as early as nine to twelve months out so you can account for shopping time, shipping, alterations, etc. Below you will find a few things to consider when choosing your wedding attire:

- Any of your ideas and inspirations
- Any cultural/religious aspects to the wedding
- The venue (e.g., getting married on a beach versus getting married inside of a house of worship)
- Your budget

If you are shopping for any type of attire that must be special-ordered (particularly a traditional wedding gown), here is a general timeline to help you plan accordingly.

- Nine to twelve months prior to wedding day: shop for and purchase the dress
- Six months prior to wedding day: purchase undergarments, accessories, and shoes
- Three to four months prior to wedding day: take care of any necessary alterations
- Two to three weeks prior to wedding: final fitting and dress pickup

**PLANNING TIP:** *Pick out your shoes and undergarments prior to your fittings to ensure accuracy!*

## ❧ Couple's Wedding Attire ❧

Keep track of what you and your partner will be wearing for each wedding-related event.

| REHEARSAL DINNER ||
|---|---|
| **PARTNER 1** | **PARTNER 2** |
| Outfit: | Outfit: |
| Shoes: | Shoes: |
| Accessories: | Accessories: |
| Notes: | Notes: |

## ◆◆ Couple's Wedding Attire ◆◆

| CEREMONY & RECEPTION ||
|---|---|
| **PARTNER 1** | **PARTNER 2** |
| Outfit: | Outfit: |
| Shoes: | Shoes: |
| Accessories: | Accessories: |
| Notes: | Notes: |

| ADDITIONAL EVENT #1 ||
|---|---|
| **PARTNER 1** | **PARTNER 2** |
| Outfit: | Outfit: |
| Shoes: | Shoes: |
| Accessories: | Accessories: |
| Notes: | Notes: |

## ✦ Couple's Wedding Attire ✦

| ADDITIONAL EVENT #2 ||
|---|---|
| **PARTNER 1** | **PARTNER 2** |
| Outfit: | Outfit: |
| Shoes: | Shoes: |
| Accessories: | Accessories: |
| Notes: | Notes: |

| ADDITIONAL EVENT #3 ||
|---|---|
| **PARTNER 1** | **PARTNER 2** |
| Outfit: | Outfit: |
| Shoes: | Shoes: |
| Accessories: | Accessories: |
| Notes: | Notes: |

# ◆◆ Couple's Wedding Attire ◆◆

| ADDITIONAL EVENT #4 ||
|---|---|
| **PARTNER 1** | **PARTNER 2** |
| Outfit: | Outfit: |
| Shoes: | Shoes: |
| Accessories: | Accessories: |
| Notes: | Notes: |

| ADDITIONAL EVENT #5 ||
| --- | --- |
| **PARTNER 1** | **PARTNER 2** |
| Outfit: | Outfit: |
| Shoes: | Shoes: |
| Accessories: | Accessories: |
| Notes: | Notes: |

# ⇥ Wedding Party Attire ⇤

Utilize the chart below to keep track of everyone's wedding-day attire to help you with your overall vision and planning.

| NAME | TITLE/ROLE | ATTIRE |
|------|------------|--------|
|      |            |        |
|      |            |        |
|      |            |        |
|      |            |        |
|      |            |        |
|      |            |        |
|      |            |        |
|      |            |        |
|      |            |        |
|      |            |        |
|      |            |        |

| NAME | TITLE/ROLE | ATTIRE |
|---|---|---|
|  |  |  |
|  |  |  |
|  |  |  |
|  |  |  |
|  |  |  |
|  |  |  |
|  |  |  |
|  |  |  |
|  |  |  |
|  |  |  |
|  |  |  |
|  |  |  |
|  |  |  |

# Accommodations

..................

Whether you are having a local wedding or a destination wedding, it will be important to both consider and plan for accommodations for your guests and wedding party. This does not necessarily mean that you will be paying for them; it means that you have done the work to ensure your guests have a safe place to stay at the end of the festivities. You can simply provide your guests with suggestions, or you can seek out a hotel block (hold a certain number of rooms), which typically allows your guests to book rooms at a discounted rate. This section will help you log the information you collect.

# ❖ Hotel Block Options ❖

| VENUE NAME | LOCATION | TYPE *(e.g., Hotel, Bed and Breakfast, etc.)* | ROOM BLOCK PRICE AND DETAILS |
|---|---|---|---|
| | | | |
| | | | |
| | | | |
| | | | |
| | | | |
| | | | |
| | | | |
| | | | |
| | | | |
| | | | |
| | | | |
| | | | |

| VENUE NAME | LOCATION | TYPE *(e.g., Hotel, Bed and Breakfast, etc.)* | ROOM BLOCK PRICE AND DETAILS |
|---|---|---|---|
| | | | |
| | | | |
| | | | |
| | | | |
| | | | |
| | | | |
| | | | |
| | | | |
| | | | |
| | | | |
| | | | |
| | | | |

# ❧ Accommodations for ❧ Distinguished Guests

The following chart will help you keep track of where everyone closest to you, such as immediate family and your wedding party, is staying. This can also include you and your partner!

| GUEST | ACCOMMODATION | WHO IS PAYING |
|---|---|---|
| | | |
| | | |
| | | |
| | | |
| | | |
| | | |
| | | |
| | | |
| | | |
| | | |

| GUEST | ACCOMMODATION | WHO IS PAYING |
|-------|---------------|---------------|
|       |               |               |
|       |               |               |
|       |               |               |
|       |               |               |
|       |               |               |
|       |               |               |
|       |               |               |
|       |               |               |
|       |               |               |
|       |               |               |
|       |               |               |
|       |               |               |
|       |               |               |

## ❖ Transportation Details ❖

Use this space to record all transportation details.

| SERVICE PROVIDER | NUMBER OF PEOPLE | COST | PICK UP AND DROP OFF |
|---|---|---|---|
|  |  |  |  |
|  |  |  |  |
|  |  |  |  |
|  |  |  |  |
|  |  |  |  |
|  |  |  |  |
|  |  |  |  |
|  |  |  |  |
|  |  |  |  |
|  |  |  |  |
|  |  |  |  |

| SERVICE PROVIDER | NUMBER OF PEOPLE | COST | PICK UP AND DROP OFF |
|---|---|---|---|
|  |  |  |  |
|  |  |  |  |
|  |  |  |  |
|  |  |  |  |
|  |  |  |  |
|  |  |  |  |
|  |  |  |  |
|  |  |  |  |
|  |  |  |  |
|  |  |  |  |
|  |  |  |  |
|  |  |  |  |
|  |  |  |  |

# Rehearsal

....................

If you and your partner are going the traditional route and plan on having a rehearsal dinner, it will certainly require some planning attention. You can also use this section to plan for a "Welcome Dinner" if that applies to your wedding weekend plans. If a pre-wedding dinner does not fit into the desired schedule, please feel free to skip through this section!

## ❖ Rehearsal Venue Options ❖

| |
|---|
| Venue: |
| Location: |
| Contact: |
| Capacity: |
| Accessibility: |
| Cost: |
| Notes: |

| |
|---|
| Venue: |
| Location: |
| Contact: |
| Capacity: |
| Accessibility: |
| Cost: |
| Notes: |

| |
|---|
| Venue: |
| Location: |
| Contact: |
| Capacity: |
| Accessibility: |
| Cost: |
| Notes: |

| |
|---|
| Venue: |
| Location: |
| Contact: |
| Capacity: |
| Accessibility: |
| Cost: |
| Notes: |

## ❖ Rehearsal Vendors ❖

| |
|---|
| Name: |
| Type (e.g., stationery, florals, etc.): |
| Contact information: |
| Cost: |
| Notes: |

| |
|---|
| Name: |
| Type (e.g., stationery, florals, etc.): |
| Contact information: |
| Cost: |
| Notes: |

| |
|---|
| Name: |
| Type (e.g., stationery, florals, etc.): |
| Contact information: |
| Cost: |
| Notes: |

| |
|---|
| Name: |
| Type (e.g., stationery, florals, etc.): |
| Contact information: |
| Cost: |
| Notes: |

## ⊷ Seating Arrangements ⊶

Use this space to plan your seating. You can use your invitee list to figure out who will be attending the rehearsal before planning seating.

| HEAD/TOP TABLE |
| --- |
|  |
|  |
|  |
|  |
|  |
|  |
|  |
|  |
|  |
|  |
|  |

| TABLE THEME/NUMBER: | TABLE THEME/NUMBER: |
| --- | --- |
|  |  |

# ❖ Seating Arrangements ❖

| TABLE THEME/NUMBER: | TABLE THEME/NUMBER: |
|---|---|
|  |  |

| TABLE THEME/NUMBER: | TABLE THEME/NUMBER: |
|---|---|
| | |

# ❧ Seating Arrangements ❧

| TABLE THEME/NUMBER: | TABLE THEME/NUMBER: |
|---|---|
|  |  |
|  |  |
|  |  |
|  |  |
|  |  |
|  |  |
|  |  |
|  |  |
|  |  |
|  |  |
|  |  |
|  |  |
|  |  |

| TABLE THEME/NUMBER: | TABLE THEME/NUMBER: |
| --- | --- |
| | |

# ❖ Ceremony Rehearsal ❖

Use the table below to plan for who will be playing a part in your ceremony and therefore will need to attend the ceremony rehearsal.

CEREMONY REHEARSAL LOCATION:

| LIST OF REHEARSAL ATTENDEES |
| --- |
|  |
|  |
|  |
|  |
|  |
|  |
|  |
|  |
|  |
|  |

| LIST OF REHEARSAL ATTENDEES |
|---|
| |
| |
| |
| |
| |
| |
| |
| |
| |
| |
| |
| |

## ⇔ Rehearsal Dinner Schedule ⇔

Use the chart below to lay out the schedule for your rehearsal and rehearsal dinner. This can include the time you rehearse, arrival times, the time dinner is being served, what time you want speeches to occur, etc.

| TITLE | TIME | NOTES, DURATION, ETC. |
|---|---|---|
| *Example: Arrival* | *5 p.m.* | *Wedding party to arrive before guests.* |
| | | |
| | | |
| | | |
| | | |
| | | |
| | | |
| | | |
| | | |
| | | |
| | | |

| TITLE | TIME | NOTES, DURATION, ETC. |
|---|---|---|
| | | |
| | | |
| | | |
| | | |
| | | |
| | | |
| | | |
| | | |
| | | |
| | | |
| | | |
| | | |
| | | |
| | | |

# Ceremony

....................

Now, it's time for us to walk through planning the ceremony. Everyone's ceremony will look different and depend on things like religious and cultural customs, personal preferences, how traditional you imagine it being, etc. Use this section to plan the ceremony of your dreams. Feel free to cross out, add, and edit anything to personalize it to your experience.

## ⊷ Questions to Consider ⊶

Here are some questions to consider with your partner as you plan out your ceremony (or ceremonies). You are also welcome to add any additional questions of your own!

- Will our officiant help guide us through our ceremony plans?
- Do our houses of worship have any requirements or things we should be aware of when planning our ceremony?
- How long do we want our ceremony or ceremonies (if applicable) to last?
- What religious/cultural aspects are important for us to include?
- What religious/cultural aspects are important to our families?
- How will we exchange rings?
- Who will hold our rings?
- How will the order of procession work? Does our processional order matter to our venue?
- What music do we want to include? How will we relay this to our music vendor?
- Will we write and read our own vows?
- Will we have any family members or distinguished guests do any type of reading or other religious/cultural demonstration?
- Do we want to have any type of moment of silence or honoring moment?

**Other:**

- _____
- _____
- _____
- _____
- _____
- _____

## ⊷ Ceremony Plans ⊶

Use this space to answer the questions on page 166 and brainstorm the flow of your ceremony. You may also want to include any décor elements here.

## ⇔ Ceremony Plans ⇔

## ✤ Processional Order ✤

Use this space to plan out your processional order.

**PLANNING TIP:** *If you are getting married in a house of worship, they may have a certain expectation for the processional order, so be sure to check before you plan.*

**Traditional Processional Order Example:**

1. Grandparents and extended family
2. Groom's parents (or just father)
3. Mother of the bride (unless both parents are walking her down the aisle)
4. Priest/officiant
5. Groom
6. Best man and maid of honor (can walk together or alone)
7. Bridesmaids and groomsmen
8. Ring bearer
9. Flower girl
10. Bride with father of the bride (or both parents)

**Our processional order:**

1. _____
2. _____
3. _____
4. _____
5. _____
6. _____
7. _____
8. _____
9. _____
10. _____

## ⇥ Vows ⇤

If you and your partner are choosing to write your own vows, use this space to brainstorm.

## ❖ Ceremony Schedule ❖

Use this chart to finalize your ceremony or ceremonies schedule. You will want to consider sharing your schedule with those who are directly involved, such as your immediate family and wedding party.

| ASPECT OF CEREMONY | TIME | NOTES AND DETAILS |
|---|---|---|
| | | |
| | | |
| | | |
| | | |
| | | |
| | | |
| | | |
| | | |
| | | |

| ASPECT OF CEREMONY | TIME | NOTES AND DETAILS |
|---|---|---|
|  |  |  |
|  |  |  |
|  |  |  |
|  |  |  |
|  |  |  |
|  |  |  |
|  |  |  |
|  |  |  |
|  |  |  |
|  |  |  |
|  |  |  |

## ✤ Ceremony Schedule ✤

| ASPECT OF CEREMONY | TIME | NOTES AND DETAILS |
|---|---|---|
| | | |
| | | |
| | | |
| | | |
| | | |
| | | |
| | | |
| | | |
| | | |
| | | |

| ASPECT OF CEREMONY | TIME | NOTES AND DETAILS |
|---|---|---|
| | | |
| | | |
| | | |
| | | |
| | | |
| | | |
| | | |
| | | |
| | | |
| | | |
| | | |

# Reception

It's time to celebrate! Similar to all of the aspects of our planning thus far, there is no one-size-fits-all recipe for the perfect reception. When you combine your and your partner's preferences, style, culture, religion, etc., your reception will be its own. Use this section as a guide to help you finalize your reception plans, schedule, and seating arrangements.

## ⊷ Traditions and Customs ⊷

Here is a list of customs that may occur during a traditional reception.

- Cocktail hour (before official reception begins)
- Newlyweds' entrance
- Newlyweds' first dance
- Other first dances (i.e., bride and father of the bride, groom and mother of the groom, etc.)
- Blessings, toasts, and speeches
- Meal
- Bouquet and garter toss
- Cake cutting
- Dancing and celebration
- Couple farewell

Use this space to brainstorm the activities and any other elements you want to ensure take place at your reception.

_____
_____
_____
_____
_____
_____
_____
_____

## ✦ Cocktail Hour ✦

If you are planning on doing a cocktail hour, this is a good place to brainstorm any specialty drink ideas, music, menus, or plans you may have for this time.

_____
_____
_____
_____
_____
_____
_____
_____
_____
_____
_____
_____
_____
_____
_____
_____
_____
_____
_____
_____
_____
_____
_____
_____
_____

# ❧ Dinner Menu ❧

Whether you are having a buffet, plated, or family style meal, use this space to plan your menu as you coordinate with your venue.

1. What type of meal style do we want for our wedding? Check what applies.
   - ○ Buffet
   - ○ Plated
   - ○ Family style
   - ○ Other _____

2. Who will be cooking/doing the food?
   - ○ Family/Friends
   - ○ Venue
   - ○ Vendor
   - ○ Other _____

3. Is the venue providing food services (e.g., staff, menu programs, etc.)? Circle what applies.

   YES   or   NO

4. How many people are we feeding (include any vendors that will be present on the day of the event)?

   _____

   _____

   _____

   _____

   _____

**Food Options for Reception:**

_____
_____
_____
_____
_____
_____
_____
_____

**Dietary Restrictions/Allergies/Notes:**

_____
_____
_____
_____
_____
_____
_____
_____

## ⇥ Music Choices ⇤

Use this space to list songs you would like played for parts of your reception, such as entrances, first dances, cake cutting, and general dancing time.

## ⤝ Speeches/Toasts ⤞

Use the space below to brainstorm who you would like to ask to speak at your reception.

| NAME | RELATIONSHIP TO US |
|------|--------------------|
|      |                    |
|      |                    |
|      |                    |
|      |                    |
|      |                    |
|      |                    |
|      |                    |
|      |                    |
|      |                    |
|      |                    |
|      |                    |

| NAME | RELATIONSHIP TO US |
|------|---------------------|
|      |                     |
|      |                     |
|      |                     |
|      |                     |
|      |                     |
|      |                     |
|      |                     |
|      |                     |
|      |                     |
|      |                     |
|      |                     |
|      |                     |

## ↔ Cake ↔

This space is dedicated to your cake and dessert planning! Write down general ideas, notes of your cake tasting, cake vendors, and more.

## ❖ Reception Schedule ❖

Use this table to plan out how you want your reception to be.

| ASPECT OF RECEPTION | TIME | NOTES AND DETAILS |
|---|---|---|
| | | |
| | | |
| | | |
| | | |
| | | |
| | | |
| | | |
| | | |
| | | |
| | | |
| | | |
| | | |

| ASPECT OF RECEPTION | TIME | NOTES AND DETAILS |
|---|---|---|
|  |  |  |
|  |  |  |
|  |  |  |
|  |  |  |
|  |  |  |
|  |  |  |
|  |  |  |
|  |  |  |
|  |  |  |
|  |  |  |
|  |  |  |
|  |  |  |
|  |  |  |
|  |  |  |

## ❈ Seating Arrangements ❈

| HEAD/TOP TABLE |
| --- |
|  |
|  |
|  |
|  |
|  |
|  |
|  |
|  |
|  |
|  |
|  |

| TABLE THEME/NUMBER: | TABLE THEME/NUMBER: |
| --- | --- |
|  |  |

## ❖ Seating Arrangements ❖

| TABLE THEME/NUMBER: | TABLE THEME/NUMBER: |
|---|---|
|  |  |
|  |  |
|  |  |
|  |  |
|  |  |
|  |  |
|  |  |
|  |  |
|  |  |
|  |  |
|  |  |
|  |  |
|  |  |
|  |  |

| TABLE THEME/NUMBER: | TABLE THEME/NUMBER: |
| --- | --- |
| | |

# Seating Arrangements

| TABLE THEME/NUMBER: | TABLE THEME/NUMBER: |
|---|---|
| | |

| TABLE THEME/NUMBER: | TABLE THEME/NUMBER: |
|---|---|
|  |  |

# Schedule

....................

Creating a schedule for your wedding day or weekend is crucial—not only to keep you and your partner organized, but also to set expectations for distinguished guests, and communicate timelines with your vendors. Now that you have a clear plan for your ceremony and reception, use this section to plan out your entire wedding day or wedding weekend. Think of it as the big picture! Once complete, send it to vendors, wedding party, immediate family, and other distinguished guests. Aim to finalize the schedule three to four weeks prior to the wedding to allow for changes. Keep in mind, you may have to consult with certain vendors to understand their schedule needs (e.g. photographer, hair and makeup, etc.) before finalizing your wedding timeline.

# ⇔ Traditional Wedding Schedule ⇔

Here is an example of a simplified traditional wedding weekend schedule that you can fill out if this is along the lines of your wedding style; if not, you can create your own wedding schedule on page 202.

**REHEARSAL**

| DESCRIPTION | DAY/TIME |
|---|---|
| Rehearsal Dinner or Other Event | |

**WEDDING DAY**

| DESCRIPTION | DAY/TIME |
|---|---|
| Hair and Makeup | |
| Photographer Arrival | |
| First Look | |
| Limo Pickup | |
| Arrival at Church | |
| Church Ceremony Begins | |
| Ceremony Concludes | |
| Couple, Family, Wedding Party Photos | |

| | |
|---|---|
| Limo Pickup for Venue | |
| Arrive at Venue | |
| Cocktail Hour | |
| Reception Begins | |
| Couple Entrance and First Dance | |
| Welcome Toast | |
| Parent Dances | |
| Dinner | |
| Toasts & Speeches | |
| Bouquet Toss/Garter Toss | |
| Cake Cutting | |
| Dancing | |
| Grand Exit/End Time | |

## DAY AFTER

| DESCRIPTION | DAY/TIME |
|---|---|
| Brunch or Other Event | |

## ◆◆ Our Wedding Schedule ◆◆

Use this space to create your wedding weekend or day schedule.

| DESCRIPTION | TIME |
|---|---|
|  |  |
|  |  |
|  |  |
|  |  |
|  |  |
|  |  |
|  |  |
|  |  |
|  |  |
|  |  |
|  |  |

| DESCRIPTION | TIME |
|---|---|
| | |
| | |
| | |
| | |
| | |
| | |
| | |
| | |
| | |
| | |
| | |
| | |

# Events

This next chart is dedicated to helping you plan for any other events that may take place on or around your wedding weekend. Whether it be a shower, welcome party, bridal brunch, afterparty, post-wedding brunch, etc., please feel free to use this chart and blank space to help you plan.

## ❧ Other Events Game Plan ❧

Use these pages to plan out any other events.

| |
|---|
| Event: |
| Host: |
| When: |
| Where: |
| Number of Guests/Children: |
| Vendors Needed: |
| Notes/Details: |

| |
|---|
| Event: |
| Host: |
| When: |
| Where: |
| Number of Guests/Children: |
| Vendors Needed: |
| Notes/Details: |

| |
|---|
| Event: |
| Host: |
| When: |
| Where: |
| Number of Guests/Children: |
| Vendors Needed: |
| Notes/Details: |

| |
|---|
| Event: |
| Host: |
| When: |
| Where: |
| Number of Guests/Children: |
| Vendors Needed: |
| Notes/Details: |

# ❖ Other Events Game Plan ❖

| | |
|---|---|
| Event: | |
| Host: | |
| When: | |
| Where: | |
| Number of Guests/Children: | |
| Vendors Needed: | |
| Notes/Details: | |

| | |
|---|---|
| Event: | |
| Host: | |
| When: | |
| Where: | |
| Number of Guests/Children: | |
| Vendors Needed: | |
| Notes/Details: | |

| Event: |
|---|
| Host: |
| When: |
| Where: |
| Number of Guests/Children: |
| Vendors Needed: |
| Notes/Details: |

| Event: |
|---|
| Host: |
| When: |
| Where: |
| Number of Guests/Children: |
| Vendors Needed: |
| Notes/Details: |

# Post-Wedding

Whether you are reading this section before your wedding or decided to wait until after the festivities, the planning is not quite finished yet! This section covers anything that you may need to take care of soon after your wedding, including your honeymoon and thank-you notes. Use this section to write out what you still need to do and your honeymoon plans, and to keep track of who needs a thank-you note.

## ⤙ Post-Wedding To-Do List ⤚

Here's a recommended list of things you may have yet to do. Feel free to skip over any of the points that you've already completed or do not apply to you. If there are any additional things you want to complete, add them here as well!

- Return any rentals
- Complete vendor payment/tips
- Send thank-you notes
- Leave vendor and venue reviews
- Freeze your wedding cake
- Clean and preserve your gown/wedding attire
- Repurpose your wedding bouquet
- Begin gathering the documents and information needed to change your last name (if this is something you have chosen to do)
- Organize wedding photos for an album
- Registry exchanges/returns
- Deposit monetary gifts
- Sit as partners to discuss next steps with finances, taxes, insurance, etc.
- Enjoy your time as newlyweds!

**Other:**

- _____
- _____
- _____
- _____

**PLANNING TIP:** *Many registry platforms will offer a discount immediately following your wedding on any item that was not purchased. If there is anything you did not receive that you really want/need, take advantage of this discount!*

# ❖ Thank-You Notes ❖

A thoughtful thank-you note is one that is handwritten, personal, specific, and full of emotion. It goes beyond simply saying "thank you." It is best to have both members of the couple sign it despite who may have written it.

You will want to send a thank-you note to:

- Wedding event attendees who brought/sent gifts (monetary or physical)
- Guest who could not attend events but sent gifts (monetary or physical)
- Your wedding party
- Anyone who played a major part in the planning process
- Anyone who financially contributed to/hosted any part of the wedding
- Vendors
- Officiant(s)
- Anyone who hosted a wedding event for you (welcome party, brunch, etc.)

**PLANNING TIP:** *While it is never too late to send a thank-you note, try to send them out no later than six to eight weeks following your wedding. If you are having a shower, shower thank-you notes should be sent as gifts arrive, or immediately following your shower.*

## ⇥ Gift List ⇤

Keep track of who got you a gift to make it easier for you when you are planning to send thank-you notes.

| NAME | GIFT | THANK-YOU NOTE (check mark) |
|---|---|---|
|  |  | ○ |
|  |  | ○ |
|  |  | ○ |
|  |  | ○ |
|  |  | ○ |
|  |  | ○ |
|  |  | ○ |
|  |  | ○ |
|  |  | ○ |
|  |  | ○ |
|  |  | ○ |
|  |  | ○ |
|  |  | ○ |

| NAME | GIFT | THANK-YOU NOTE *(check mark)* |
|---|---|---|
| | | ○ |
| | | ○ |
| | | ○ |
| | | ○ |
| | | ○ |
| | | ○ |
| | | ○ |
| | | ○ |
| | | ○ |
| | | ○ |
| | | ○ |
| | | ○ |
| | | ○ |
| | | ○ |
| | | ○ |
| | | ○ |

## Gift List

| NAME | GIFT | THANK-YOU NOTE (check mark) |
|---|---|---|
| | | ○ |
| | | ○ |
| | | ○ |
| | | ○ |
| | | ○ |
| | | ○ |
| | | ○ |
| | | ○ |
| | | ○ |
| | | ○ |
| | | ○ |
| | | ○ |
| | | ○ |
| | | ○ |

| NAME | GIFT | THANK-YOU NOTE *(check mark)* |
|---|---|---|
|  |  | ○ |
|  |  | ○ |
|  |  | ○ |
|  |  | ○ |
|  |  | ○ |
|  |  | ○ |
|  |  | ○ |
|  |  | ○ |
|  |  | ○ |
|  |  | ○ |
|  |  | ○ |
|  |  | ○ |
|  |  | ○ |
|  |  | ○ |
|  |  | ○ |
|  |  | ○ |

# ❖ Honeymoon Planning ❖

If you are planning your honeymoon, utilize this space to collect your research and determine your initial plans.

**Money Collected (if using a honeymoon fund):** $_____

**Total Budget:** $_____

**Potential Destinations:**

- _____
- _____
- _____
- _____
- _____
- _____
- _____
- _____
- _____
- _____
- _____
- _____
- _____
- _____

# ❖ Honeymoon Itinerary ❖

Enter all of your honeymoon reservation details here.

| |
|---|
| Destination: |
| Hotel: |
| Check-In Date: |
| Check-Out Date: |
| Transportation: |
| Planned Activities/Excursions: |
| Notes: |

## ❧ Love, Laughter, and Happily Ever After! ❧

Here are my quick tips and tricks to keep in mind while planning your big day.

- Don't forget to take care of yourself throughout the planning process. While it is an extremely exciting time, it can also be stressful and emotional.

- Staying organized and getting ahead of things will pay off in the end.

- If things begin to get overwhelming, don't underestimate the power of delegating tasks!

- Leave a cushion for your miscellaneous and unexpected costs. They will come up!

- Use your timeline to help you stay on track with the big picture. It's easy to get lost in the details.

- Don't rush into any decisions you are unsure of! Sleep on things and trust your gut feeling.

- Take thorough notes during meetings, tours, and brainstorming sessions. It will be a lot of information to take in.

- Much of your vendor communication will take place via email but be sure to also have a face-to-face or virtual meeting to ensure nothing gets lost in email communication.

- Read vendor and venue contracts in detail before signing them.

- Put your vendor tips in labeled envelopes before the wedding so they are easily distributable.

- Start your beauty regimens early (at least six months in advance) so you have plenty of time to try different things out and find experts that you trust.

- Ensure that you have a clear plan for eating on the day-of! Things will get busy with getting ready, photographs, the actual event, etc.

- Break in your new wedding shoes!

- Don't forget to prepare your "wedding day emergency" kit and have it easily accessible. Your kit can include items such as deodorant, Band-Aids, lip gloss, a sewing kit, extra phone chargers, over-the-counter medications, hairspray, etc.

- Remember the true reason for this special day!

## Notes

© 2025 by Quarto Publishing Group USA Inc.
Text © 2025 by Mariah Grumet Humbert

First published in 2025 by Rock Point, an imprint of The Quarto Group,
142 West 36th Street, 4th Floor, New York, NY 10018, USA
(212) 779-4972 www.Quarto.com

All rights reserved. No part of this book may be reproduced in any form without written permission of the copyright owners. All images included in this book are original works created by the artist credited on the copyright page, not generated by artificial intelligence, and have been reproduced with the knowledge and prior consent of the artist. The producer, publisher, and printer accept no responsibility for any infringement of copyright or otherwise arising from the contents of this publication. Every effort has been made to ensure that credits accurately comply with information supplied. We apologize for any inaccuracies that may have occurred and will resolve inaccurate or missing information in a subsequent reprinting of the book.

Rock Point titles are also available at discount for retail, wholesale, promotional, and bulk purchase. For details, contact the Special Sales Manager by email at specialsales@quarto.com or by mail at The Quarto Group, Attn: Special Sales Manager, 100 Cummings Center Suite 265D, Beverly, MA 01915 USA.

10 9 8 7 6 5 4 3 2 1

ISBN: 978-1-57715-494-5

Digital edition published in 2025
eISBN: 978-0-7603-9386-4

Library of Congress Cataloging-in-Publication Data
Names: Grumet Humbert, Mariah, author.
Title: The essential wedding planner : every checklist, tool, and tip needed to plan the perfect day / Mariah Grumet Humbert.
Description: New York, NY : Rock Point, 2025. | Summary: "The Essential Wedding Planner offers an efficient and elegant place for engaged couples to organize their thoughts, ideas, and plans to execute their perfect day"—Provided by publisher.
Identifiers: LCCN 2024046765 (print) | LCCN 2024046766 (ebook) | ISBN 9781577154945 (hardcover) | ISBN 9780760393864 (ebook)
Subjects: LCSH: Weddings—Planning.
Classification: LCC HQ745 .G785 2025 (print) | LCC HQ745 (ebook) | DDC 392.52—dc23/eng/20241008
LC record available at https://lccn.loc.gov/2024046765
LC ebook record available at https://lccn.loc.gov/2024046766

Group Publisher: Rage Kindelsperger
Editorial Director: Erin Canning
Creative Director: Laura Drew
Senior Art Director: Marisa Kwek
Managing Editor: Cara Donaldson
Senior Acquiring Editor: Nicole James
Editor: Keyla Pizarro-Hernández
Interior Design: Howie Severson

Printed in China